THE **SEX**

CONSPIRACY

Winning the Battle Against Sexual Temptations

TONY O. AKPATI

The Sex Conspiracy
The First Edition 2013
Copyright @ 2013 Anthony O. Akpati

ISBN 978 0991 364107

Unless otherwise noted, all scripture is from the New King James Version of the Bible © 1982 by Thomas Nelson, Inc. Used by permission. Scripture quotations marked KJV are from the King James Version of the Bible.

Cover Design and Layout by
MYPRO DESIGN - 214 228-4278

The King's House Publications
The King's House Ministries
P. O. Box 860214
Plano TX 75074
Email: info@thekingshouselive.org
Email: info@gospelpowerbooks.com
Website: www.thekingshouselive.org

Dedication

To the glory of the Lord, I am dedicating this my first book to my Father in the Lord and mentor, Bishop David O. Oyedepo. I am thankful to God for the privilege of encountering you and your ministry in my life's journey. Papa, I lack adequate words to convey my heart's gratitude to God for sending you to our generation. Thank you for all you do for the sake of the kingdom of God.

Acknowledgement

I give God all the glory for the supply of the Spirit of Jesus Christ that made the writing of this book possible. I want to say thank you to my wife Paulina, my children Israel, Daniel and Precious, for their patience, love and support. I want you to know that you are a vital and indispensable part of this project. I love you all.

I want to say a special thank you to Daddy G.O, the General overseer of the Redeemed Christian Church of God worldwide, Pastor Enoch A. Adeboye. Daddy you have been a blessing to me, my family and ministry. My family and I are among the partakers of the grace of God upon your life. Thank you for the privilege.

I want to say special thanks to all those who have been supporting us in the work of the ministry through their fellowship, giving and prayers.

I also want to thank Pastors Ajibike and Bunmi Akinkoye of Redeemed Christian Church of God NA, Pastors John and Ibi Omewah of RCCG Heaven's Glorious Embassy, Plano Texas USA, Pastors Jude and Dorcas Akinleyimu of Christian Faith and Fellowship Mission, Dallas Texas USA, for the opportunity given me to do the work of the ministry, for their prayers and encouragement.

Also Pastor and Mrs. Chris Adetoro, Pastor and Mrs. Israel Ekundayo, Pastor and Mrs. Cornelius Oyelami, Pastor and Mrs. Joseph Omosigho, and Pastor and Mrs. Tunde Adebiyi who have all been of great blessing to me and my family. Thank you.

Sister Felicia Ojemaye, Sister Pat Agolua and Sister Nkechi Ekezie, my big sisters, I really appreciate you all. Thank you for being a blessing.

My appreciation also goes to Sister Joy Ntibundu who edited this work, Pastor Taiwo Ayeni who proofread it, critiqued and made some critical corrections, brother Gbenga Olowo who designed the cover, and sister Funmi Olowo, who made the final correction.

Finally, I want to thank Pastor Sunday Omotosho, for his unrelenting encouragement and prayers, and the success team for their support and prayers. God bless you.

Foreword

I cannot remember ever reading a book that bluntly addressed the issue of ungodly sexual practices like this before. Not only did it address the issue, it provided a practical approach to dealing with it, and I have no doubt this is from the Spirit of God.

Every chapter of this book will challenge and inspire you to strive to please God in all that you do, especially in your approach to the issue of sex. God's original plan concerning sex was that it should be enjoyed between husband and wife. Like every other thing that God created, the devil is all out to change its purpose.

The moment you begin to read this book you won't be able to put it down until you get to the last page. Above all I believe God will use this book as an instrument of deliverance in the lives of many and as a guide to a life of sexual purity to as many as will apply its message to their lives. This book is a must-read for every man and woman. Also, I will recommend this book for our young adults.

Pastor John Omewah
Senior Pastor, RCCG, Heaven's Glorious Embassy,
Plano, Texas USA

TABLE OF CONTENTS

WISDOM NUGGET
(INTRODUCTION)

"There is no beautiful war anywhere in the world. Every war is intended for the opposition to suffer loss and casualties."- Bishop David Oyedepo

INTRODUCTION

"And the lords of the Philistines came up to her and said to her, "Entice him, and find out where his great strength lies, and by what means we may overpower him, that we may bind him to afflict him; and every one of us will give you eleven hundred pieces of silver." Judges 16:5

Before you read the rest of this book I would like to inform you that there is a conspiracy in hell against your life. The devil and his agents have plotted to frustrate your purpose. One of their secret plans towards accomplishing their goal is getting you to engage in illegitimate sexual practices. If you are a keen observer you will notice that there is a deadly plague spreading all over the whole world. This plague is more dangerous than cancer, it is another holocaust, and it is the plague of sexual sin. An evil vacuum engine has been turned on, which is threatening to suck in everything on its path, it is sexual sin.

Whether you choose to believe it or not, the earth's atmosphere has been sexually polluted. There is no safe haven anywhere in the world. Whether you are black or white, Christian or non Christian, clergy or a lay person you are vulnerable. The conspiracy is strong and it has no regard for race, color, gender, religious or political affiliation. No one is exempted from this diabolical assault from the kingdom of darkness, and without Christ as a very present help, the battle will be one sided.

"And war broke out in heaven: Michael and his angels fought with the dragon; and the dragon and his angels fought, but they did not prevail, nor was a place found for them in heaven any longer. So the great dragon was cast out, that serpent of old, called the Devil and Satan, who deceives the whole world; he was cast to the earth, and his angels were cast out with him." (Revelation 12:7-9)

We are facing an epic battle in this end-time. The war that started in heaven among angels has extended to the earth and has now involved humanity. Does it surprise you why almost every commercial on the media today, both electronic and print, carries a sexual undertone? This is the strategy of the kingdom of darkness, in their aggressive pursuit of the agenda of hell to taint man with sin, make him susceptible to God's judgment, and have him dethroned from his God given position.

The kingdom of darkness, has confederated and conspired with the forces of darkness, that one of the best ways they could attack and destroy humanity is through man's sexuality. Think about all that is going on in the world today regarding sex and sexuality. Think of all the hypes and controversies about the subject of sex. Then you will come to the same conclusion that it is not ordinary. There is a spiritual influence behind it all, and Satan is that influence.

"For we wrestle not against flesh and blood, but against principalities, against powers, against the rulers of darkness of this world, against spiritual wickedness in high places." Ephesians 6:12

Bishop David Oyedepo of the Living Faith Bible Church Ota Nigeria, once said, "There is no beautiful war anywhere in the world. Every war is intended for the opposition to suffer loss and casualties." The devil is on a mission *"to steal, to kill and to destroy"* John 10:10a. The kingdom of darkness has unleashed unclean spirits to pollute as many as they can, in order to take them captive, destroy their lives here on earth, and their souls in eternity. Unfortunately, you hardly hear about this issue, and in the few places you hear about it, the emphasis is lacking. Yet, this is an issue we deal with everyday. I have good news for you. You can overcome them. I am confident that you will win in this battle.

"You are of God, little children, and have overcome them, because He who is in you is greater than he who is in the world." 1 John 4:4

Another reassuring passage of scripture declares,

"For whatsoever is born of God overcomes the world, and this is the victory that overcomes the world, even our faith". 1 John 5:4

What you will read from this book is not what somebody made up. It is a distinct sound of the trumpet of the watchman, receiving instructions from his Commander, the Lord Jesus Christ.

The duty of the watchman is to alert the people about any impending danger. I also am *"a man subject to like passion,"* as you are (James 5:17). The fact that I am the humble vessel he has prepared and chosen to use to publish it (Ps 68:11), does not make me any different. We all live in the same world. The same adversary that is seeking your life is seeking mine too. But do not fear, just follow me on this matter as I follow Jesus, and it shall be well with you.

"Stay with me; do not fear. For he who seeks my life seeks your life, but with me you shall be safe." (1 Samuel 22:23)

You can only overcome through Christ Jesus. You need to abide in him or else the devil will sweep you off your feet.

"Nor is there salvation in any other, for there is no other name under heaven given among men by which we must be saved." (Acts 4:12)

May I let you know at this point that this book is not a quick fix to the endemic problem of sexual temptations and sexual sins, neither is it a 'one to seven step' process of getting free from sexual temptation. Rather, it is a call to a life of consecration. The life of consecration puts you in check so that the devil does not take advantage of your natural propensity to do evil, which is in every man.

Beware

Sexual temptation did not start today. It has been around even in the Bible days. You met it here when you were born and it will still be around long after you are gone.

"And it came to pass after these things, that his master's wife cast her eyes upon Joseph; and she said, Lie with me. But he refused, and said unto his master's wife, Behold, my master wotteth not what is with me in the house, and he hath committed all that he hath to my hand; There is none greater in this house than I; neither hath he kept back anything from me but thee, because thou art his wife: how then can I do this great wickedness, and sin against God? And it came to pass, as she spake to Joseph day by day, that he hearkened not unto her, to lie by her, or to be with her. And it came to pass about this time, that Joseph went into the house to do his business; and there was none of the men of the house there within. And she caught him by his garment, saying, Lie with me: and he left his garment in her hand, and fled, and got him out."
Genesis 39:7-12 (KJV)

Right from the Bible days till today, men have had to learn by bitter experiences, the sting of sexual temptation. We don't need to add to the statistics. We don't have to wait until tragedy happens in order to learn. Many generals in God's army have been wounded, and many have fallen. Are you strong? You are not as strong as Samson. He had a prophetic destiny and the gift of supernatural strength. His birth was announced by an Angel. He single-handedly destroyed the whole army of the Philistines, but ended up a victim of sexual temptation (Judges 15 & 16).

Are you a wise man? Solomon was the wisest man that ever lived on the face of the earth, yet he fell into the trap of sexual temptation and ended up with seven hundred wives and three hundred concubines (1Kings 11:1-3), contrary to God's commandment.

Do you love God? King David was a man singled out for his love for God. He was so passionate for God and his kingdom that the Bible described him as *"a man after God's heart"* Acts 13:22. He also fell into the same trap of sexual temptation. We need men like Joseph who can forfeit their coats *"......than enjoy the pleasures of sin for a season."* Hebrews 11:25.

Listen to what Solomon has to say:

*"My son, pay attention to my wisdom; Lend your ear to my understanding, That you may preserve discretion, And your lips may keep knowledge. For the lips of an immoral woman drip honey, And her mouth is smoother than oil; But in the end she is bitter as wormwood, Sharp as a two-edged sword. Her feet go down to death, Her steps lay hold of hell. Lest you ponder her path of life - Her ways are unstable; You do not know them. Therefore hear me now, my children, And do not depart from the words of my mouth. **Remove your way far from her, And do not go near the door of her house**, Lest you give your honor to others, And your years to the cruel one; Lest aliens be filled with your wealth, And your labors go to the house of a foreigner; And you mourn at last, When your flesh and your body are consumed, And say: "How I have hated instruction, And my heart despised correction!*

I have not obeyed the voice of my teachers, Nor inclined my ear to those who instructed me!" Proverbs 5:1-13. The emphasis is mine.

Stand your ground, and refuse to compromise with the enemy and God will give you victory in Jesus name. You will never regret it in Jesus name. The writer of the book of Hebrews challenged our attitude in dealing with sin when he said,

"Ye have not yet resisted unto blood, striving against sin." Hebrews 12:4.

Therefore, do all you can to resist to the end and like Joseph, win the battle against sexual temptation. Furthermore, it is my prayer that the Almighty God will keep you from falling, and grant you the grace to keep yourself unspotted from sin and the world in Jesus name. Amen!

> *"Living a life independent of God, no matter how glamorous it appears from human perspective, is a disaster in the making"*

CHAPTER 1

UNDERSTANDING
TEMPTATION

T he Greek word *peirasmos* translated as temptation, is the same word used for trial or test. In other words, this same word has two different meanings in its usage. Therefore, it is important for us to distinguish between the two forms of usage. In one form, it implies a persuasion or enticement to do evil, which in other words means temptation. This is exactly what we face on a daily basis, and the Chief Architect behind it is Satan or the Devil. He is called the Tempter, (in the gospel of Matthew 4:3), and the Accuser of the Brethren (in Revelation 12:10).

Satan wants to enslave man and take away his inheritance. His ultimate desire is to turn man away from following God, and to destroy his relationship with God. He instigates every desire or action contrary to the word of God. The sum total of the temptations we face is to get us to the point where we have to choose between what makes sense, and what God says, with the intension to make us violate the commandments of God.

"The thief does not come except to steal, and to kill, and to destroy. I have come that they may have life, and that they may have it more abundantly." John 10:10

The greatest lie ever told by the devil is that man can live independent of God. Living a life independent of God, no matter how glamorous it appears from human perspective, is a disaster in the making. Man was created to be God-dependent, just the same way the tree was created to depend on the soil, or the fish on water. The Lord Jesus exemplified this truth during the time of his temptation.

"But He answered and said, "It is written, 'Man shall not live by bread alone, but by every word that proceeds from the mouth of God." Matthew 4:4

Our words, our thoughts and our actions, everything about man was to be determined and influenced by the word of God. When the serpent came into the garden of Eden, he did not attack Adam and Eve, he attacked the word of God in their lives. The exact same thing we are experiencing today.

"Now the serpent was more cunning than any beast of the field which the LORD God had made. And he said to the woman, "Has God indeed said, 'You shall not eat of every tree of the garden'? And the woman said to the serpent, "We may eat the fruit of the trees of the garden; but of the fruit of the tree which is in the midst of the garden, God has said, 'You shall not eat it, nor shall you

touch it, lest you die. Then the serpent said to the woman, "You will not surely die. For God knows that in the day you eat of it your eyes will be opened, and you will be like God, knowing good and evil." Genesis 3:1-5

The devil deceived the woman to believe that God was being unnecessarily restrictive and convinced her to her own shame and disgrace, that she could live independent of God. Her husband joined her in that delusion. This cost them the beautiful Garden of Eden, and they were stripped of dignity and honor.

What we have today as liberal movement all over the world, that man has the right to choose to live the way he wants, started from Eden. Freedom without boundaries will always lead to captivity and destruction. Freedom is not doing what you like; it is doing what is right in the sight of God. Freedom should only be exercised within the confines of the word of God.

"All things are lawful for me, but not all things are helpful; all things are lawful for me, but not all things edify." 1 Corinthians 10:23

God did not give us his word because he wants to put restrictions on us. He gave us his word to prepare and preserve a people of destiny, because of his love for us.

19

"For this is the love of God, that we keep His commandments. And His commandments are not burdensome." 1 John 5:3

As long as we live in this world, temptations will always be there because the devil is still around. Yet God wants us to overcome at all times.

Test or Trial

As mentioned earlier, on the other hand, the word *peirasmos* also means trial or test. Most of the time this talks about the temporal or momentary painful experiences, persecutions, conflicts, difficulties, and confrontations the Lord allows to come our way in order to test our obedience to him, and mature us as his followers. It is sometimes called the trial of faith. Someone once said that "obedience that is not tested is not true obedience." The obedience test is the proof of your love for God and loyalty to his word. Jesus said,

"If ye love me, keep my commandments" (John 14:15 KJV).

The whole account of the book of Job is a case of trial allowed by God.

"Now there was a day when the sons of God came to present themselves before the LORD, and Satan came also among them.

And the LORD *said unto Satan, Whence comest thou? Then Satan answered the* LORD*, and said, From going to and fro in the earth, and from walking up and down in it. And the* LORD *said unto Satan, Hast thou considered my servant Job, that there is none like him in the earth, a perfect and an upright man, one that feareth God, and escheweth evil? Then Satan answered the* LORD*, and said, Doth Job fear God for nought? Hast not thou made an hedge about him, and about his house, and about all that he hath on every side? thou hast blessed the work of his hands, and his substance is increased in the land. But put forth thine hand now, and touch all that he hath, and he will curse thee to thy face. And the* LORD *said unto Satan, Behold, all that he hath is in thy power; only upon himself put not forth thine hand. So Satan went forth from the presence of the* LORD*."* Job 1:6-12 (KJV)

We also read in Genesis chapter twenty-two beginning from verses one to three:

Now it came to pass after these things that God tested Abraham, and said to him, "Abraham!" And he said, "Here I am." Then He said, "Take now your son, your only son Isaac, whom you love, and go to the land of Moriah, and offer him there as a burnt offering on one of the mountains of which I shall tell you." So Abraham rose early in the morning and saddled his donkey, and took two of his young men with him, and Isaac his son; and he split the wood for the burnt offering, and arose and went to the place of which God had told him."

In verses ten to twelve, of the same chapter the Bible states:

"And Abraham stretched out his hand and took the knife to slay his son But the Angel of the Lord called to him from heaven and said, "Abraham, Abraham!"So he said, "Here I am." And He said, "Do not lay your hand on the lad, or do anything to him; for now I know that you fear God, since you have not withheld your son, your only son, from Me."

In another passage of scripture, we read:

"And you shall remember that the Lord your God led you all the way these forty years in the wilderness, to humble you and test you, to know what was in your heart, whether you would keep His commandments or not." Deuteronomy 8:2

Another way the word 'tempt' is used in the Bible, which is also a form of test or trial is when as humans, we tempt God by disregarding his instructions. Whether we believe it or not, every violation of scripture carries a consequence. Unknown to many is the fact that the law of God is spiritual. The fact that there is no tangible manifestation of consequence when you violate the word of God does not mean that nothing happened, neither does it absolve you of the consequences.

Also, people tempt God by acting on the word of God based on assumptions. Sometime ago, a man in Africa jumped into a lion's cage because he claimed to be a prophet, and that the God that delivered Daniel of the Bible will also deliver him.

It is a pity he never lived to tell the story, because the hungry lions devoured him in minutes. Taking unreasonable and irrational risk that is uncalled for will be tempting God and jeopardizing one's life. The devil said to Jesus:

"If You are the Son of God, throw Yourself down. For it is written: 'He shall give His angels charge over you, 'and, 'In their hands they shall bear you up, Lest you dash your foot against a stone." (Matthew 4:6)

"Nor let us commit sexual immorality, as some of them did, and in one day twenty-three thousand fell; nor let us tempt Christ, as some of them also tempted, and were destroyed by serpents." (1 Corinthians 10:8-9)

Things To Note About Temptation

- You are not the only one being tempted. Everyone is faced with it, you are not alone. (1 Corinthians 10:13)

- It is not a strange phenomenon (1 Peter 4:12)

- Your temptation is not special; other individuals are going through the same experience, there is nothing new under the sun. (1 Peter 5:9)

- It has a purpose, it will not leave you the same way it met you. It can be a viable tool in the hand of Satan for destruction, if you give in to it, and a formidable weapon of growth and maturity in God's hand, if you resisted the enemy.

- The outcome of every temptation depends on your choice.

- Temptation is not sin in itself, yielding to it, is.

- The enemy takes advantage of the daily seasons of life, when you are hungry, angry or alone, to tempt you.

Stages of Temptation

"Let no one say when he is tempted, "I am tempted by God;" for God cannot be tempted by evil, nor does He Himself tempt anyone. But each one is tempted when he is drawn away by his own desires and enticed. Then, when desire has conceived, it gives birth to sin; and sin, when it is full-grown, brings forth death." (James 1:13-15)

From the above passage of scriptures we can distinguish three stages of temptation. The first stage is the drawing away or enticement stage. This is the onset of temptation. It is the stage of attraction. It is the time a person's heart is attracted to something ungodly. It is the time the enemy wants to plant the evil seed in form of thoughts in a person's heart. It is the image formation level. It is a time the enemy wants you to shift the focus of your mind from what is healthy and helpful to what is toxic and destructive to your soul. The devil tries to bring all kinds of perverted desires and ideas into your mind. At this level you can easily turn down the offer of the devil without much struggle, by guarding your mind and refusing any evil thought to stay.

"Finally, brethren, whatever things are true, whatever things are noble, whatever things are just, whatever things are pure, whatever things are lovely, whatever things are of good report, if there is any virtue and if there is anything praiseworthy—meditate on these things." Philippians 4:8

Ask yourself, "Is there any virtue in what I am thinking?" "Is it praiseworthy?" If not, don't allow that thought to stay. Interrupt that thought process immediately. Thoughts are like seeds, if you allow them, they will grow. It takes one thought to displace another. If you can't think of any thought to displace a negative or an evil thought, think on the cross of Jesus. The book of Colossians declares in verse two of chapter three,

"Set your mind on things above, not on things on the earth."

You can experience enticement and yet refuse to be enticed.

"My son, if sinners entice thee, consent thou not. If they say, Come with us, let us lay wait for blood, let us lurk privily for the innocent without cause: Let us swallow them up alive as the grave; and whole, as those that go down into the pit: We shall find all precious substance, we shall fill our houses with spoil: Cast in thy lot among us; let us all have one purse: My son, walk not thou in the way with them; refrain thy foot from their path." - Proverbs 1:10-15 (KJV)

It is all the battle of the mind which is a form of spiritual warfare. Don't allow the enemy to sow the seed of evil thought in your heart. God spoke through prophet Haggai in the book of Haggai chapter one in verse five and said

"Now therefore, thus says the LORD *of hosts: "Consider your ways!"*

Pay attention to the thought that is going on in your mind. Stop any evil thought going on in your mind, because if you can't stop the thought, you can't stop the act. Ask yourself a soul searching question, "Is there any profit in this thing I am thinking about"?

"For as he thinks in his heart, so is he." "Eat and drink!" he says to you, But his heart is not with you." (Proverbs 23:7)

"Keep your heart with all diligence, For out of it spring the issues of life." Proverbs 4:23

If you delay your action or refuse to act at this point, the enemy will push you down to the second level, making it harder for you to come out from that temptation as we see in the case of King David.

" And it came to pass, after the year was expired, at the time when kings go forth to battle, that David sent Joab, and his servants with him, and all Israel; and they destroyed the children of Ammon, and besieged Rabbah. But David tarried still at Jerusalem. And it came to pass in an eveningtide, that David arose from off his bed, and walked upon the roof of the king's house: and from the roof he saw a woman washing herself; and the woman was very beautiful to look upon. And David sent and enquired after the woman. And one said, Is not this Bathsheba, the daughter of Eliam, the wife of Uriah the Hittite? And David sent messengers, and took her; and she came in unto him, and he lay with her; for she was purified from her uncleanness: and she returned unto her house. And the woman conceived, and sent and told David, and said, I am with child. And David sent to Joab, saying, Send me Uriah the Hittite. And Joab sent Uriah to David." - 2 Samuel 11:1-6 (KJV)

This whole event in the life of king David that led to the killing of a loyal and dedicated servant, a humble and innocent man, could have been avoided if he had acted at the initial stage of the temptation. Job said,

"I have made a covenant with my eyes; Why then should I look upon a young woman?" (Job 31:1)

Refuse to dwell on the thoughts the enemy wants you to dwell on. Counter his suggestions with, "it is written," speaking God's Word back to him.

The second stage is when one's imagination has been trapped in the magnetic field of the evil one, with a perverted thought pattern. And as the person begins to browse in his own mind the web page of evil desires, then the lust of the flesh, the lust of the eyes, and the pride of life immediately take hold of his or her heart. The person then begins to fantasize in his or her mind, "How delicious this apple will be in my mouth!" He or she begins to desire the evil the enemy is projecting into his or her mind. Such a person has been overtaken by the deceitfulness of sin. Yet the word of God does not approve of that for us as his children.

"We know that we are of God, and the whole world lies under the sway of the wicked one." 1 John 5:19

At this stage you have dwelt long enough on the destructive land mines of evil thought that the enemy is putting in your mind. When you allow an unclean thought into your mind, it controls your life and you become powerless against it. There are things to think on and there are things not to think on as we are counseled in Philippians 4:8.

"Finally, brethren, whatever things are true, whatever things are noble, whatever things are just, whatever things are pure, whatever things are lovely, whatever things are of good report, if there is any virtue and if there is anything praiseworthy—meditate on these things."

Any thought that will not enhance your relationship with God or edify your life and make you a better person is not worth dwelling on for a second. Do away with it immediately. It is in the second stage of temptation that you will practically experience the battle between the soul and the spirit of God in you. This is something you do not want to experience. It is easier to fight an offensive battle than to fight a defensive one.

For example, no one goes to the store to buy trash. We buy what we need in our homes. But in the process we generate trash. That's why we have trash cans in our homes. Think about the number of times you have to empty the trash in a week. Honestly, they fill up so quickly, and if you don't take them out, you are toying with a costly health hazard! You must do to filthy thoughts in your mind the same thing you do to the garbage - trash them.

Similarly, the computers, by design have delete buttons and recycle bins or else, our work will be full of errors and typos. So also, some of the thoughts that come through your mind are not what you planned. You have heard the saying "You cannot stop a bird from flying across your head, but you can stop it from building a nest on your hair".

In the same way you should create an imaginary trash bin or delete button in your mind. When an evil or unclean thought comes, because you can't stop it from coming, you can do away with it by vehemently resisting it.

"Submit yourselves therefore to God. Resist the devil and he will flee from you." (James 4:7).

You are the one that decides whether it stays or not. You can say it out loud, "This one goes to the trash or recycle bin." You have the right and ability to control your mind. No one can do that for you.

"Whoever has no rule over his own spirit is like a city broken down, without walls." (Proverbs 25:28)

The third stage of temptation is when the enemy has overpowered the person. This is the stage of obsession. The person has lost control of his or her life to the enemy. Imagine a car in motion with a failure in its breaking system, without divine intervention, that car is bound to crash. So it is with this stage of temptation. The person doesn't have the ability to put up any resistance against the devil anymore. The enemy has succeeded in pushing the person into a pit. Whatsoever he wants he or she to do at this point is the exact thing he or she will do. At this point, the person needs help to come out of that evil web of the enemy. Don't wait until you drown. Be humble enough to confide in your pastor, a trustworthy brother or sister, a dependable man or woman of God who will agree with you in prayer.

"Confess your faults one to another, and pray one for another, that ye may be healed. The effectual fervent prayer of a righteous man availeth much." - James 5:16 (KJV)

There is something powerful about confession, that it breaks the back of the enemy, so that he can't stand. This makes him lose his grip over one's mind. Don't listen to his lies. Confess it and you will expose him and there will be no place for him to hide. The enemy is vicious, when you cover it up, he will ensnare you. When he ensnares you, you become addicted and he will take over the control of your life.

At some other time in this stage, when you call on God in your distress, God by his mercy restores his Spirit in you, and enables you to fight and recover your lost ground. After Samson's hair was shaven, after some time, *"....the hair of his head began to grow again...."* (Judges 16:22).

"And Samson called unto the LORD, and said, O Lord God, remember me, I pray thee, and strengthen me, I pray thee, only this once, O God, that I may be at once avenged of the Philistines for my two eyes." (Judges 16:28)

"Do you not know that to whom you present yourselves slaves to obey, you are that one's slaves whom you obey, whether of sin leading to death, or of obedience leading to righteousness?" (Romans 6:16)

One of the main tools the enemy uses in enslaving his victims is deception. He presents a lie to them for the truth. He justifies their sinful practices and gives them reasons to continue in the path of sin and destruction. Sometimes he backs up his lies with the word of God, and shows them some human examples to reinforce his lies. Instead of turning to God in humility and repentance, they become bold in their sin, not knowing that the enemy is out to destroy their lives.

Don't give the devil any room to operate in your life, *nor give place to the devil.* (Ephesians 4:27). The good news is that through Jesus Christ, you can take back any place the devil has taken in your life.

WISDOM NUGGET 2

> *"When Satan comes with his temptation, he embellishes it with pleasure to make it attractive and irresistible."*

CHAPTER 2

DO NOT START
THE FIRE

"Do not lust after her beauty in your heart, Nor let her allure you with her eyelids. For by means of a harlot A man is reduced to a crust of bread; And an adulteress will prey upon his precious life. Can a man take fire to his bosom, And his clothes not be burned? Can one walk on hot coals, And his feet not be seared?" (Proverb 6:25-28)

In one of our safety huddles in my place of work, we extensively discussed fire safety and awareness. I learned several lessons about fire and fire safety which are helping me to be safety-conscious both at work and at home. Not only that, I found its application in my spiritual life also helpful. A spark or a little fire is capable of causing an inferno which can consume everything around.

In my work place they treat a spark the same way they will treat a fire. When there is a spark, they call in the Fire Department for proper evaluation and documentation. They do taproot investigation for the root cause, and they come up with corrective and preventive measures. This is serious!

The one that intrigued me most was the fire triangle. This talks about the three elements that come together before a fire can start. They are oxygen, combustible materials and an ignition source. The absence of any of these elements means the absence of fire. In the work place, we have no control over oxygen, because there is air everywhere. As much as we want to control combustible materials, we still have them around since we need them to do our job. The ignition source is the only one we can control. Most of the weight of our fire preventive activities lies more towards controlling the ignition source.

The best way to prevent a fire is to not start one. There are things we ought to do if we desire not to start the fire of sexual passion. Do not initiate any relationship that will not enhance your relationship with God. Ask yourself, "What is the purpose of allowing this close relationship?" "What is in it for me?" If you cannot establish the purpose, the intimacy is uncalled for. This is because what starts as a harmless relationship can be hijacked and perverted by the enemy and made to have a sexual undertone, and before long you will be struggling with sexual temptation.

You need to guard your space and don't let anyone encroach into your life. It is enough battle to ward off the arrows of lust and temptations flying all around through what we see and hear, do not bring one into your life. I say this to the men, be careful how you compliment a woman that is not your wife. Do not say to her, your voice sounds like that of an angel.

I am sure you have never heard an angel speak before. Do not say to her "You are too pretty," - reserve that for your wife. I believe you have heard the statement "The way women are wired is different from the way men are wired." Have you?

What you assume to be a casual complimentary statement, innocently made, the woman takes to heart. She will subconsciously 'regurgitate' that statement, chew it over and over until the 'amplified version' of the simple statement is formed. She will interpret it to mean that you are a nice person and you are kind and caring, even though you are unaware of the fire you just ignited.

Then because she loves what she is hearing, she keeps coming back to the source of her passion. This is because a woman does not only hear words, she feels every word she hears, whether complimentary or derogatory. Because what you said is passionately appealing to her, she begins to compare you with her husband who does not compliment her in that manner. Therefore, for this reason she wants to reciprocate your kind gesture, and a serious, but unintentional bond is formed in the process. Then, your trouble has just begun.

Most immoral relationships begin in the manner described above. Hence, watch what you say or do and do not keep any secret relationship, with the opposite sex. Do not go near sexual sin, it is epidemic. What it is doing in peoples' lives, homes and families is devastating. Avoid undefined relational proximity to a woman or vice versa, such relational proximity will erode every atom of resistance in you toward sexual temptation. It does not matter how strong you think you are, when you stay too long around sexual temptation you will become its next victim.

Do not think that you are strong, or that you can handle that, or that you know the limit you can go. Remember 1 Corinthians 10:12:

"Wherefore let him that thinketh he standeth take heed lest he fall."

It is the lie of the devil to think you can handle sexual temptation in your own power. The only antidote to sexual temptation that is clearly and unambiguously mentioned in the Bible is *"Flee fornication....."* (1 Corinthians 6:18). And also 1 Thessalonians 5:22: *"Abstain from all appearance of evil."*

Having silly, deceptive self confidence against sexual temptation is one of the easiest ways the devil keeps you from fighting back when he attacks. Before you get to that limit, he will push you overboard, and you will be wondering, what has happened?

"For she has cast down many wounded, And all who were slain by her were strong men." (Proverbs 7:26)

"nor give place to the devil." (Ephesians 4:27)

It is very easy to start a fire, but it takes a whole lot to put it out. Anywhere there is a fire incident, there is always destruction, it doesn't matter how little. What a man labored to build all his life can be destroyed by one act of indecent behavior. Your life is like building a tower, one block at a time. If you mess up, you will crash.

You can socialize, and yet not get entangled. This is why we need wisdom from God to be able to draw a line between interaction and temptation. Do not trust your heart, you don't know what you are capable of doing until you are exposed to certain situations.

"The heart is deceitful above all things, And desperately wicked; Who can know it?" (Jeremiah 17:9)

Why should you trust in something the word of God says is desperately wicked? Only trust in the living word of God. When Satan comes with his temptation, he embellishes it with pleasure to make it attractive and irresistible (Hebrews 11:25). He chooses a delivery mode that will appeal to you. Remember, he is the wise serpent (Matthew 10:16). You don't use sugar as a bait in trap intended to catch a rat. Satan knows his business. If Satan would show himself for what he truly is, and what he represents, people can easily avoid him. What he presents to you for pleasure is actually a trap in disguise. It is a bait to catch one into destruction.

"And no wonder! For Satan himself transforms himself into an angel of light." (2 Corinthians 11:14)

" lest Satan should take advantage of us; for we are not ignorant of his devices." (2 Corinthians 2:11)

He hides the devastating consequences that come with yielding to his temptation from you, and amplifies the pleasure side of it. Many have fallen to his tricks over and over again.

"Immediately he went after her, as an ox goes to the slaughter, Or as a fool to the correction of the stocks, Till an arrow struck his liver. As a bird hastens to the snare, He did not know it would cost his life." (Proverbs 7:22-23)

"Stolen water is sweet, And bread eaten in secret is pleasant. But he does not know that the dead are there, That her guests are in the depths of hell. (Proverbs 9:17-18)

Any time you come under the attack of temptation, let it be clear to you that the enemy has desired to steal from you. It may be your peace or your joy, or something else. He has desired to kill or destroy something you cherish. There is no idle time with him. He exploits every opportunity that comes his way. He means business and goes all out in pursuit of his wicked agenda. It could be one's marriage, health, finances or some other things, and when these happen, be sure he is out for you with his evil devices. Counter attack immediately, because delay can be dangerous.

"A prudent man foresees evil and hides himself, But the simple pass on and are punished." (Proverbs 22:3)

Be on your guard; Stand your Ground

"Be sober, be vigilant; because your adversary the devil walks about like a roaring lion, seeking whom he may devour." (1 Peter 5:8)

Your most unguarded moment is likely the time the enemy will strike. The enemy is going around looking for whom he will destroy. When he comes around, and sees you unguarded, he strikes without wasting time. No crack in a fortress should be ignored. The slightest opening you create for the enemy is enough for him to come in and wreak havoc.

"nor give place to the devil" (Ephesians 4:27)

When you give the devil a foot-hold, he turns it to a stronghold. The enemy is looking for an opportunity to make you fall. Do not give him that opportunity.

"but while men slept, his enemy came and sowed tares among the wheat and went his way." (Matthew 13:25)

This speaks of spiritual complacency. When you lose sight of the fact that you are in a perpetual conflict with the evil one, and you begin to handle the issues of your life with laxity, and you begin to toy with sin, then you give the enemy the opportunity to invade your life. Be warned!

"There is a fault line in every man as a result of the fall. Born again or not, anointed or not, there lies buried beneath the fabrics of our mortal flesh, the fallen old nature."

CHAPTER 3

NO MORE PLAYING IN
THE DEN

T he den is the stronghold of the lion. Any animal that steps into the den can as well be considered dead. All through history the only man that came out alive from the lion's den was Daniel. In his case, he did not walk in there by himself; he was unjustly thrown into the lion's den but God rescued him. To think that you can walk into 'lion's den' and come out unscathed will be self deception.

The den in this case is a sexually pervaded setting, or sexually attractive person, which or who may stir up sexual passion in you. You are not made of stones, even when man was comparatively referred to as a stone in the Bible, God qualifies it with the adjective, "lively". In other words, you are active and full of life.

" Ye also, as **lively** stones, are built up a spiritual house, an holy priesthood, to offer up spiritual sacrifices, acceptable to God by Jesus Christ." - 1 Peter 2:5 (KJV)

Do not put yourself in a position where you will be found struggling to keep your body in check. You won't understand how vulnerable you are until you are exposed to certain environment. Don't try it! It is always too late by the time you discover your vulnerability in the den, you are already in the belly of the lion. The corroborative account of Lot's experience in Sodom and Gomorrah, and the outcome is graphically described in 2 Peter 2:8:

"(for that righteous man, dwelling among them, tormented his righteous soul from day to day by seeing and hearing their lawless deeds)"

There is a fault line in every man as a result of the fall. Born again or not, anointed or not, there lies buried beneath the fabrics of our mortal flesh, the fallen old nature. That is why the Bible instructs us to run away anytime we are faced with sexual temptation, or else we cave in and fall like a pack of cards. Hanging around the den is a dangerous game, because it will ignite sexual passion. Once sexual passion is ignited, it becomes difficult for you to resist the temptation.

There is something Paul the apostle referred to as the "... *infirmity of the flesh...*" in the book of Romans chapter six in verse nineteen. He was not speaking of sickness, but weakness of the flesh. If you subject any material to certain conditions, after some time the integrity of that material will fail and the ability to resist stress will not be there anymore.

In the same way, anyone that is exposed to the den for a prolonged period of time is susceptible to fall due to sexual pressures and stress.

The flesh will always want you to do something that will bring you down, so be careful. That's why the scripture rightly says, according to the book of Romans chapter thirteen in verse fourteen,

"But put on the Lord Jesus Christ, and make no provision for the flesh, to fulfill its lusts."

Solomon from his wealth of experience, after acquiring a thousand women for himself alone (1 Kings 11:3), has this to say:

*"There are three things which are too wonderful for me, Yes, four which I do not understand: The way of an eagle in the air, The way of a serpent on a rock, The way of a ship in the midst of the sea, **And the way of a man with a virgin.**"* (Proverbs 30:18-19)

The emphasis in the above scripture is called chemistry in some circles. You can't just explain it, but there is a stirring up, and an attraction between a man and a woman, and a bond begins to form. Every attempt made by Samson's parents to discourage him from hanging around the 'den' fell on deaf ears. He refused to heed their instructions until his eyes were plucked out.

"Now Samson went down to Timnath, and saw a woman in Timnath of the daughters of the Philistines. So he went up and told his father and mother, saying, "I have seen a woman in Timnath of the daughters of the Philistines; now therefore, get her for me as a wife." Then his father and mother said to him, "Is there no woman among the daughters of your brethren, or among all my people, that you must go and get a wife from the uncircumcised Philistines?" And Samson said to his father, "Get her for me, for she pleases me well." (Judges 14:1-3)

Do not play around sexual sin, it can floor any man. Jesus said, *".....the flesh is weak."* (Matthew 26:41). It cannot withstand the pressure that comes from sexual temptation. The Bible did not mince word regarding sexual temptation, and its alluring or captivating effect. It says,

"Can a man take fire to his bosom, And his clothes not be burned?" (Proverbs 6:27)

If you don't burn outwardly by your actions, you burn inwardly through lust. Both of these are weapons of destruction in the hands of the enemy. The Bible goes on to say, in the book of first Thessalonians in chapter five verse twenty-two, *"Abstain from every form of evil"*

That is to say keep away from it, don't hang around it. By all means, avoid any sexually provocative setting. Do not keep company with a woman that is not your wife, especially in private. Do not visit a single lady living alone by yourself unaccompanied.

Avoid being in the dark with a woman that is not your wife. Also put away pornography and sexually explicit materials from you. The natural inclination or the default position of the flesh due to the fall of man is sensual pleasure; exposing it to such environment will not be to its advantage. Samson, with all his anointing died as a fool would, with his eyes plucked out, simply because he played in the den.

"Now therefore, listen to me, my children; Pay attention to the words of my mouth: Do not let your heart turn aside to her ways, Do not stray into her paths; For she has cast down many wounded, And all who were slain by her were strong men. Her house is the way to hell, Descending to the chambers of death." (Proverbs 7:24-27)

The new birth, or being born again, does not change the flesh from what it is. It is only our spirit that is reborn at salvation. All the old natural tendencies are still locked up in the flesh. It is only self-discipline, training and renewing of the mind with the word of God that can make you to overcome the dictates of the flesh.

"He who comes from above is above all; he who is of the earth is earthly and speaks of the earth. He who comes from heaven is above all." (John 3:31)

The flesh is of the earth, and it will naturally delight in doing earthly things. Paul the Apostle said,

"But I discipline my body and bring it into subjection, lest, when I have preached to others, I myself should become disqualified," (1 Corinthians 9:27).

In conclusion you have to practically restrain the flesh from having its way. Avoid inappropriate relational proximity, define your relationship, and set up the boundaries.

WISDOM NUGGET 4

> *"Many have sold their ultimate for the immediate pleasure of sex."*

CHAPTER 4

EXCHANGING YOUR DESTINY
FOR SEX

Everyone is born into this world with a destiny to fulfill. Everyone is born into this world on purpose. There is no one without a purpose. It does not matter the way you were born into this world, in wedlock or out of wedlock, or as a result of a rape, God has a purpose and a plan for your life. As a matter of fact, purpose is the first thing any manufacturer considers before making any product. The fact that you were born is enough evidence that you have a purpose.

Man is an exclusive product of God. We did not just appear out of the blue. Man did not metamorphose from apes, it does not matter our morphological and physiological closeness to those of apes.

"And God said, Let us make man in our image, after our likeness: and let them have dominion over the fish of the sea, and over the fowl of the air, and over the cattle, and over all the earth, and over every creeping thing that creepeth upon the earth.

So God created man in his own image, in the image of God created he him; male and female created he them." - Genesis 1:26-27 (KJV)

"Know that the Lord, *He is God; It is He who has made us, and not we ourselves; We are His people and the sheep of His pasture."* (Psalm 100:3)

God made everyone, and he gave us the body we have for a purpose. Hear what he says:

"Now the body is not for sexual immorality but for the Lord, and the Lord for the body." (1 Corinthians 6:13b)

"For I know the thoughts that I think toward you, says the Lord, *thoughts of peace and not of evil, to give you a future and a hope."* (Jeremiah 29:11)

"Before I formed you in the womb I knew you; Before you were born I sanctified you; I ordained you a prophet to the nations." (Jeremiah 1:5)

Your destiny is part of the glory of God in your life, and it is meant for you to shine in this world. Every one born into this world has a divine deposit, a gift from God, the resources of heaven invested in him or her. No one is born just to make up the number of human beings on earth. Every attack of the enemy upon a man's life whether directly or indirectly is targeted towards removing this glory and replacing it with shame and reproach.

Whenever the enemy sees the star of any man, his next agenda will be how to destroy that star. When Jesus was born and his star was seen, the devil stirred up Herod to try to destroy him. One of the most gruesome infanticides ever recorded in human history, was carried out by Herod in his attempt to destroy Jesus.

There is a strong conspiracy in the kingdom of darkness to destroy mankind through sexual contamination. The only way they want to accomplish this is by making men and women to engage in illegitimate sexual practices, that is, sex outside God's design. Premarital sex, adultery, shack up and homosexuality are all forms of illegitimate sexual practices. Any sexual practice outside the creator's order is an abuse of sex. God gave man the gift of sex for a purpose. It is for intimacy, procreation, and for mutual enjoyment of the man and his lawfully married wife.

According to the Creator's design, a man is not permitted to go into a woman without marital commitment. God's standard is zero tolerance for premarital sex. Abuse should not be a norm, we should be willing and determined to make a change. To sleep with a woman that is not your wife "...*is an heinous crime, it is iniquity to be punished by the judges.*" (Job 31:9-11). Sex in marriage is the only safe sex; it is not the use of contraceptives and condoms. The cultures we live in have bought into the lie of the devil, and they promote it at all cost. God has not changed his mind neither has he reviewed his word. His standard is still the same, let no man deceive you.

"And He answered and said to them, "Have you not read that He who made them at the beginning 'made them male and female,' and said, 'For this reason a man shall leave his father and mother and be joined to his wife, and the two shall become one flesh?" (Matthew 19:4-5)

Many have fallen victim to the plot of the enemy and have sold their birthrights just like Esau, when he came under the pressure of hunger, and sold his birthright for a morsel of bread. Unknown to them, the enemy throws in a bargain any time he comes with sexual temptation. He offers you sex in exchange for your destiny, the great plan of God for your life. Many have sold their ultimate for the immediate pleasure of sex. Illegitimate sex is not for free, you might not know this. Any time a person engages in illegitimate sex, he or she is giving up something of eternal value. You might not offer money, but you are giving up something, though intangible, yet it is inestimable.

*"Then he turned to her by the way, and said, "Please let me come in to you"; for he did not know that she was his daughter-in-law. So she said, "**What will you give me, that you may come in to me?**"*
*And he said, "I will send a young goat from the flock." So she said, "Will you give me a pledge till you send it?" Then he said, "What pledge shall I give you?" So she said, "Your **signet and cord, and your staff** that is in your hand." Then he gave them to her, and went in to her, and she conceived by him."* (Genesis 38:16-18)

The signet and cord, and your staff implies your spirit and soul, and your body. The devil is saying, hand over your destiny to me, and give me the control of your life. Little wonder the Bible says,

"Flee fornication. Every sin that a man doeth is without the body; but he that committeth fornication sinneth against his own body" (1 Corinthians 6:18).

Immorality is the only sin that impacts the three realms of a man's life, the spirit, soul and body. The devil wants you to mortgage your destiny, jeopardize your future, and give up a significant part of your blessing. Reuben lost his double portion inheritance as the firstborn of Israel because he *"...lay with Bilhah his father's concubine...." (Genesis 35:22).*

Not only is sexual sin a sin against God, it truncates a man's destiny. It makes one veer from the course of his or her life without knowing it. Your destiny is more important than sex, don't throw away your glorious destiny. The life of Joseph demonstrated the fact that when the devil offers you sex, he wants you to trade your destiny for it. As a young boy, Joseph dreamt and saw himself as a ruler or a king. On two different occasions he dreamt the same dream in two different forms. It was a vision of God for his life. It was a clear picture of his future.

"And he said unto them, Hear, I pray you, this dream which I have dreamed: For, behold, we were binding sheaves in the field, and,

my sheaf arose, and also stood upright; and, behold, your sheaves stood round about, and made obeisance to my sheaf. And his brethren said to him, Shalt thou indeed reign over us? or shalt thou indeed have dominion over us? And they hated him yet the more for his dreams, and for his words. And he dreamed yet another dream, and told it his brethren, and said, Behold, I have dreamed a dream more; and, behold, the sun and the moon and the eleven stars made obeisance to me. And he told it to his father, and to his brethren: and his father rebuked him, and said unto him, What is this dream that thou hast dreamed? Shall I and thy mother and thy brethren indeed come to bow down ourselves to thee to the earth?

And his brethren envied him; but his father observed the saying." - Genesis 37:6-11 (KJV)

"And it came to pass after these things, that his master's wife cast her eyes upon Joseph; and she said, Lie with me. But he refused, and said unto his master's wife, Behold, my master wotteth not what is with me in the house, and he hath committed all that he hath to my hand; There is none greater in this house than I; neither hath he kept back any thing from me but thee, because thou art his wife: how then can I do this great wickedness, and sin against God?

And it came to pass, as she spake to Joseph day by day, that he hearkened not unto her, to lie by her, or to be with her.

And it came to pass about this time, that Joseph went into the house to do his business; and there was none of the men of the house there within. And she caught him by his garment, saying, Lie with me: and he left his garment in her hand, and fled, and got him out." - Genesis 39:7-12 (KJV)

He esteemed his God-given destiny more than sex. That was why he was able to refuse the offer of illegitimate sex from Potiphar's wife. The worth you place on the destiny God has for you will determine how you handle it. But Esau despised his birthright.

"And Jacob sod pottage: and Esau came from the field, and he was faint: And Esau said to Jacob, Feed me, I pray thee, with that same red pottage; for I am faint: therefore was his name called Edom. And Jacob said, Sell me this day thy birthright. And Esau said, Behold, I am at the point to die: and what profit shall this birthright do to me? And Jacob said, Swear to me this day; and he sware unto him: and he sold his birthright unto Jacob. Then Jacob gave Esau bread and pottage of lentiles; and he did eat and drink, and rose up, and went his way: thus Esau despised his birthright." - Genesis 25:29-34 (KJV)

When you see what you were born to do, it becomes easy for you to resist sexual temptation, because you have something more important than the temptation. Your destiny is precious, don't throw it away. The book of Proverbs declares:

"It is an abomination to kings to commit wickedness: for the throne is established by righteousness." Proverbs 16:12 (KJV)

If you must sit on the throne of your destiny which God has for you, you must refuse sexual temptation. I need to mention at this point the fact that there are principalities living in some personalities.

You will see them as normal human beings because it is not written on their faces. They are actually evil, seductive, and destructive spirits that disguise themselves and take on the veil of the human flesh. If you mess around such personalities, you are doomed forever. God abhors illegitimate sex, and it is improper for God's children. The ultimate of your destiny is to return home to your maker and find a place in his kingdom.

"Do you not know that the unrighteous will not inherit the kingdom of God? Do not be deceived. Neither fornicators, nor idolaters, nor adulterers, nor homosexuals, nor sodomites, nor thieves, nor covetous, nor drunkards, nor revilers, nor extortioners will inherit the kingdom of God." (1 Corinthians 6:9-10)

If you desire to get to the final destination of your destiny in Christ, you must keep away from illegitimate sex. It is one of the sins that will keep some people from entering God's kingdom of heaven.

"Beloved, now we are children of God; and it has not yet been revealed what we shall be, but we know that when He is revealed, we shall be like Him, for we shall see Him as He is. And everyone who has this hope in Him purifies himself, just as He is pure."
(1 John 3:2-3)

WISDOM NUGGET **5**

"The will of God in anyone's life is not automatic. It does not run on auto pilot. If you don't desire it and if you don't allow the will of God in your life, it will not be done."

CHAPTER 5

KNOWING
GOD'S WILL

The will of God concerning sex and sexuality and every other issue of man's life is not hidden, neither is it complicated. God made it plain in the pages of the Bible. Why many people struggle with the will of God today is because they hold tightly to their own will, that seeks to gratify the flesh and satisfy the lust of their hearts. To be able to do the will of God you must surrender your own will to his will.

"For this commandment which I command you today is not too mysterious for you, nor is it far off. It is not in heaven, that you should say, 'Who will ascend into heaven for us and bring it to us, that we may hear it and do it?' Nor is it beyond the sea, that you should say, 'Who will go over the sea for us and bring it to us, that we may hear it and do it?' But the word is very near you, in your mouth and in your heart, that you may do it."
(Deuteronomy 30:11-14)

His will is that you abstain from sin. I remember an incident that occurred when I was in the university. There was this hostel mate of mine, his room was a room away from mine. One day, I was in the common room with other hostel mates when he walked in. One of the guys with us, his room-mate to be precise, told him that a lady came to look for him. He asked for her name and the guy told him. The moment his room-mate mentioned the lady's name he screamed, "Oh, I have missed this lady again." Then he added, "If it is God's will that I will sleep with this lady, she will come back again." I responded spontaneously, "It is not the will of God for you to commit fornication." Even if she the lady had come back, that would not mean it was the will of God. Even though we all lived like that at one time or the other, that does not make it God's will.

The Bible clearly states,

"And the times of this ignorance God winked at; but now commandeth all men everywhere to repent" (Acts 17:30 KJV).

One of the earliest lessons the Holy Spirit taught me after my salvation was on the subject of consecration. One day, I was studying my Bible during my quiet time and was reading Paul's letter to the Ephesians. In chapter five verse three it reads:

"But fornication, and all uncleanness, or covetousness, let it not be **once named** among you, as becometh saints" (KJV), emphasis mine.

The Holy Spirit said to me that those things should not be mentioned any more in my life, not even for one more time, now that I have become a child of God. Now, that did not stop the temptations from coming, but I made up my mind that day to stick with the will of God revealed to me. I made a vow of consecration unto the Lord after that encounter. Many times children of God are quick to blame the devil, but the main problem is their reluctance to act based on the word of God. Hear what Paul the Apostle has to say:

"But I discipline my body and bring it into subjection, lest, when I have preached to others, I myself should become disqualified" (1 Corinthians 9:27).

Paul accepted the responsibility to discipline his body. There is no gift of discipline, it is acquired through training and exercising of the mind. God will not do for you what he has given you the ability to do. For an example, God will not think for you because he has given you the brain to think.

What is the will of God?

The will of God is the word of God, and the word of God is the will of God. God wants his will to be done in our daily lives consistently and continuously. While teaching his disciples to pray, Jesus said:

"When you pray, say: Our Father in heaven, Hallowed be Your name. Your kingdom come. Your will be done On earth as it is in heaven." (Luke 11:2)

The will of God in anyone's life is not automatic. It does not run on auto pilot. In other words, it does not just happen in one's life because it is the will of God. God does not force his will on anyone. It does not get into you by just sitting around, and then like the process of osmosis, it flows into you. You have to take the responsibility to make it happen. If you don't desire it, and if you don't allow the will of God in your life, it will not be done. For example, God *"....wills that all men be saved...."* (1 Timothy 2:4), but if a person rejects God's offer for salvation, he or she will not be saved.

Someone once told me that if it was the will of God for him to stop consuming alcohol to the point of stupor that God had the power to do just that. Let me say this, God does not work according to his power, He works according to his word. He gave man the power to choose. He will be violating his word if he goes around trying to control everybody. He has given us his word, the onus is upon us to act upon the word to make the will of God manifest in our lives.

God's word had the power to create this whole world that we live in, but it will not accomplish anything in the life of a person that rejects it and refuses to apply it in his or her life. If the apostles of Christ did not act on his word, there would be no Acts of the Apostles in the Bible, says Smith Wigglesworth.

The issue of the application of the word of God is a non-negotiable matter. It is so crucial that we see it in Mathew 18:18 where we are encouraged to exercise it.

"Assuredly, I say to you, whatever you bind on earth will be bound in heaven, and whatever you loose on earth will be loosed in heaven."

That is to say, whatever you allow to happen in your life will definitely happen, and the ones you don't allow will not happen. Until you commit yourself to do his will you will not be able to do it. It takes investment to be committed. Sacrifice is the only measure of commitment. Invest your time and resources in your pursuit of God, to find out what His will is for you. Read, study and meditate on the word of God.

"Then Jesus said to His disciples, "If anyone desires to come after Me, let him deny himself, and take up his cross, and follow Me." (Matthew 16:24)

That word "deny himself," means to deprive self of those rights, and privileges that will not allow him to wholly obey or do the will of God. In other words, you purposely restrict 'self' from having its way.

"For this is the will of God, your sanctification: that you should abstain from sexual immorality; " (1 Thessalonians 4:3). Another scripture declares:

"Flee also youthful lusts; but pursue righteousness, faith, love, peace with those who call on the Lord out of a pure heart." (2 Timothy 2:22)

I want to assure you that the word of God works. All that is required of you is to take a decision to practice the instructions of the word. If the instruction of the word says run, then do just that. Jesus said in the book of John chapter seven in verse seventeen.

"If anyone wills to do His will, he shall know concerning the doctrine, whether it is from God or whether I speak on My own authority."

That is to say, the only way you can validate the word of God in your life is by practicing its instructions. Then you will know that the word of God really works. Make up your mind and make the word of God a priority in your life.

"The generations after you do not have to do what you did to suffer the consequences of your choices, or enjoy the blessings thereof. The fact that they descended from you connects them to the consequences or the blessings."

CHAPTER 6

A MATTER OF
CHOICE

"I call heaven and earth as witnesses today against you, that I have set before you life and death, blessing and cursing; therefore choose life, that both you and your descendants may live." (Deuteronomy 30:19)

One of the greatest gifts that God ever gave to man is the gift of choice. This makes it man's responsibility to make decisions. Life is full of choices. Every day we are faced with alternatives to choose from. You can choose to pray, or watch the news, or surf the web, or watch movies. The Angels of God in their magnificent beauty, splendor and power do have the privilege of making choices. Unfortunately, a lot of people have abused this privilege, and turned again to blame God. The way anyone lives his or her life is a direct product of the choices he or she had made. In other words, the choices we make turn around to make us.

The choices you make today control your present, and decide your future. Therefore, it becomes imperative for you to know what to choose in life. God made man a free will moral agent. The will is a God-given force that is able to determine its choice and habits. We are humans, not robots; we have the will power to say no to any offer we don't want. Choice-making is inevitable in life; your decision not to make a choice is a choice in itself. God placed in every man what it takes to overcome sexual temptation, but whether you overcome or not, is your choice.

Responsibility of choice-making

God gave man the right to choose and even advised him to make the right choices. Choice-making is a personal non-transferable responsibility of man. You cannot hold anyone responsible for the choices you made. Whatever you decide to do is your business, but be sure of this, there is an implication to every choice you make. You can choose to smoke, drink alcohol, do drugs, live immorally, or you can choose to live a decent and godly life. The law of seedtime and harvest is always in operation as long as this earth stands.

"While the earth remains, Seedtime and harvest, Cold and heat, Winter and summer, And day and night Shall not cease."
(Genesis 8:22)

"Do not be deceived, God is not mocked; for whatever a man sows, that he will also reap." (Galatians 6:7)

You cannot make your choice and escape the consequence that goes with it. It comes as a complete package, the choice and its consequence. Anyone that chooses to smoke may end up with lung cancer if he or she refuses to change that habit. A sexually promiscuous person will end up with sexually transmitted disease if he or she continues with that habit. A pot smoker or a drug addict will end up losing his or her mind and end up losing everything he or she has labored for, and eventually end up in the streets or in jail. The choices you make have greater impact than you think. They do not only affect you, they affect your family and generations after you.

*"For as by **one man's disobedience many were made** sinners, so also by **one Man's obedience many will be made righteous**."* Romans 5:19. (The emphasis is mine).

The generations after you do not have to do what you did to suffer the consequences of your choices, or enjoy the blessings thereof. The fact that they descended from you connects them to the consequences or the blessings. Have you ever wondered why they ask for your family history when you visit the hospital? It is the spiritual law of inheritance. If children should continue in the same choice path as their parents, they only hasten the consequences or the blessing of those choices, as the case may be. When you make good and godly choices, you and generations after you will enjoy the blessings of God.

The key to making choices

The key to making a good choice amongst many alternatives is your ability to identify what is beneficial to you. The consequences of making a wrong choice are grievous, and can be devastating. The pain you end up with by making a wrong choice by far outweighs the pleasure you derive from it.

"Choosing rather to suffer affliction with the people of God than to enjoy the passing pleasures of sin." (Hebrews 11:25)

There are so many things you might think are cool to do, but in the real sense of it, by doing those things you are destroying yourself and cutting your life short. One of such things is illegitimate sex.

"All things are lawful for me, but all things are not helpful. All things are lawful for me, but I will not be brought under the power of any." (1 Corinthians 6:12)

The modern societies' cultures and traditions negate the word of God. They call evil good, and good evil. In all that the modern society does, it wants to circumvent the law of God. The scribes and Pharisees came to Jesus and said:

"Why do Your disciples transgress the tradition of the elders? For they do not wash their hands when they eat bread." He answered and said to them, "Why do you also transgress the commandment of God because of your tradition?" (Matthew 15:2-3)

The fact that something is lawful does not make it beneficial to you. For one to be able to escape the trap of sexual temptation, he or she must be skillful in choice making. To be skillful in choice making you must arm yourself with true and relevant information. The quality of choice one makes is dependent upon the information process available to him or her. When you have the wrong information you will definitely make the wrong choice.

Unfortunately, many source their information about life only from the television screen, other news and social media, the internet, and the things they see and experience in the culture they live in. Information from these sources more often than not, is inconsistent and unreliable. This is because culture is dynamic and it changes with time. What is culturally acceptable today can become politically incorrect tomorrow. Culture has to do with the geographical location, it is not universal. What is culturally acceptable in one country can be considered an abomination in another.

Furthermore, at the other end of the spectrum of the information process is the proven truth, and the never changing word of God. It is universal and everlasting. It does not diminish or change with time. What God says in the United States of America is what he says in Europe. The same thing he also says in Africa, Asia, and Australia. It cannot be influenced or altered by the Beijing conference, the Geneva convention, the G8 summit, the United States Congress, or the government of any country in the world.

You can bank on any information you obtain from God's source. Your choice therefore, should wisely be made based on truth not on facts, emotions or feelings.

Do you know that something can be a fact and yet not be the truth? It is a fact that if I am sick I should see a doctor and take the medication he or she prescribes in order to be healed, but the truth is that my healing actually took place two thousand years ago as 1 Peter 2:24 confirms:

" - *by whose stripes you were healed.*"

Not by whose stripes, you would be healed! This truth must be embedded in your heart, to resist the fact that you are sick. Any choice you therefore made based on the truth of God's word delivers its promises and secures your future. If you choose to stand on the word of God for continuous health, financial blessings, divine favor, mercy and grace, deliverance from sexual predators and temptations, you will receive your desires.

Similarly, any one that wants to escape the man-hunt of sexual predators, diligently supervised by seducing spirits must choose what God says above every belief, ideology or opinion of any man dead or alive! For example, complete abstinence is God's choice for the unmarried, period. There is no middle ground. So your prayer should be "Lord, grant me the grace to make the choice to always honor you in my body, as long as I live, that your name alone may be glorified. Amen!"

> "Strategy helps you to prepare and to know what to do at the appropriate time. If you are not prepared you won't know what to do when the time comes."

CHAPTER 7

DEVICE YOUR
STRATEGY

A ny man that wishes to be free and stay free from sexual contamination must have a well defined strategy. If you don't have a strategy you cannot win in any battle. In fact, to engage in any battle without adequate strategy will be like one playing a game of chance. There is a popular saying that supports the need for strategizing. "He who fails to plan, plans to fail." Therefore, be wise and plan to strategize because effective strategy produces effective result.

In addition, strategy helps you to prepare and to know what to do at the appropriate time. If you are not prepared you won't know what to do when the time comes. Hear the words of Jesus profoundly reiterating the same issue:

"For which of you, intending to build a tower, does not sit down first and count the cost, whether he has enough to finish it —
lest, after he has laid the foundation, and is not able to finish, all who see it begin to mock him, saying, 'This man began to build and was not able to finish'?

Or what king, going to make war against another king, does not sit down first and consider whether he is able with ten thousand to meet him who comes against him with twenty thousand? Or else, while the other is still a great way off, he sends a delegation and asks conditions of peace." (Luke 14:28-32)

It is not the size of an army that determines its victory in any battle, but the strategy it employs. You must come up with your personal strategy that will work for you. The strategy that will help you win in this battle is not "a one size fits all," although we may have some common grounds.

I was listening to the testimony of a young man sometime ago on TBN (Trinity Broadcasting Network), who used to be a victim of drug abuse. After narrating his ordeal of years of misfortune, torture and torment in the hands of the evil one, he ended his testimony with how God rescued him. He said in his story that God delivers some people from such bondage by taking away the appetite for drugs from them, but he said that in his own case God did not take away the appetite, but rather he, on his own, came up with the strategy of accountability. He said he did not go anywhere by himself alone, even to pick mail from the box, that somebody had to go with him. Today, he is free from the bondage of drugs, and God is using him to help others who have the same problem.

The devil wants to sustain an evil pattern in the life of every man. In case you do not know, he is a crafty task master who lures his victims till they are destroyed. The good news however, is that you can be free and stay free if you choose to, because God is on your side. You must be practically involved in securing your sexual destiny. Nothing happens by chance. Anything you see happen is made to happen. The book of Hebrews chapter three verse four declares,

"For every house is built by someone, but He who built all things is God."

The surest strategy that is guaranteed to preserve any man, and prevent him from becoming a victim of sexual temptation is the strategy that is based on the word of God. It has been proven over and over again. If you must win in this battle, you must partner with God, and be ready to take his prescription.

Physical therapy is good but it has a very big limitation, it cannot handle the problem of sin. Sin is rooted in the heart, it is a spiritual sickness. You cannot use a physical approach to solve a spiritual problem. Science and medicine have no clue to the problem of sin.

"How can a young man cleanse his way? By taking heed according to Your word. With my whole heart I have sought You; Oh, let me not wander from Your commandments! Your word I have hidden in my heart, That I might not sin against You."
(Psalm 119:9-11)

True freedom and victory can only come from the hands of Jesus Christ, the word of God. If you are not willing to do something for your freedom from sexual temptation, like any other temptation, there is little or nothing anyone can do to help you. The application of the word of God was what rescued Joseph from the hands of the sexually aggressive woman, Potiphar's wife (Genesis 39). She was speaking to him the language of love from a heart of lust.

"The mouth of an immoral woman is a deep pit; He who is abhorred by the LORD will fall there." (Proverbs 22:14)

Joseph did the exact thing that God enjoins everyone of us to do when faced with sexual temptation. He ran as fast as his feet could carry him. If you refuse to run away from sexual temptation you will be dragged into compromise. You need the strength of character and the integrity of heart to do the word of God. A while ago, I received a word from God that has since made a difference in my walk of faith with him. I have been tremendously helped. And this word has become one of the most lethal amour in my spiritual armory,

"Surely in vain the net is spread in the sight of any bird;", (Proverbs 1:17).

Any time I sense that my heart is being drawn away to the things that destroy men, I quickly fire the word missile. Sometimes, I speak that scripture within me, but most of the time I verbalize it.

The most dangerous thing you can do to yourself, with regard to sexual temptation, is to lie to yourself and pretend that it does not exist.

In addition to standing on the word as a strategy, you can also vow unto the Lord not to defile your body through illegitimate sex. Vow comes from the desire and motivation to honor and please the Lord. The thirty-first chapter of the book of Job is the chapter on vows. Job vowed a vow of consecration in verses nine through to twelve.

If mine heart have been deceived by a woman, or if I have laid wait at my neighbour's door; Then let my wife grind unto another, and let others bow down upon her. For this is an heinous crime; yea, it is an iniquity to be punished by the judges. For it is a fire that consumeth to destruction, and would root out all mine increase. Job 31:9-12(KJV)

When a vow is in place the question 'should I do it or not', will not be there. God honors your vow and it is binding on you. You must be willing and determined to keep it. This is because Satan has vowed to stop any one from living a consecrated life, therefore you cannot afford to do less. This being the case you also need a vow to counter him, because it takes a vow to cancel a vow.

An oath is binding when made. When you enter the realm of oath in your quest for purity, you silence the devil. Do it voluntarily, and it will preserve your destiny in Jesus name.

"For men indeed swear by the greater, and an oath for confirmation is for them an end of all dispute." (Hebrews 6:16)

Be careful what you see

There is a children's sing-along song that says, "So be careful little eyes what you see...." I bet you know that song should not just be for children only, but more importantly, it should be for adults as well. For the men I will say, be careful how you look at a woman that is not your wife. Jesus said:

"But I say to you that whoever looks at a woman to lust for her has already committed adultery with her in his heart." (Matthew 5:28)

If you take that second look, or look for too long you will be heading towards harboring lust, then consequently you begin to lust. Lust begins in the eyes, if you don't stop it, it goes into the heart and sin is born.

"And it came to pass after these things that his master's wife cast longing eyes on Joseph, and she said, "Lie with me."
(Genesis 39:7)

When lust begins in the eyes, it spills over to the heart.

"Mine eye affecteth mine heart because of all the daughters of my city." - Lamentations 3:51 (KJV)

Whatever you feed your eyes with will definitely affect your heart. Job said,

"I have made a covenant with my eyes; Why then should I look upon a young woman? (Job 31:1).

You have the responsibility of controlling your eye gates. I believe one of the reasons why the neck is equipped with a pivot joint is for us to be able to rotate our head in order to change our gaze when we want to. More so, the eyelids do not only protect the eye balls, they help us to shut away unwanted images. God help me!

WISDOM NUGGET **8**

> *"As long as a man wants to please the flesh and gives it all that it craves for, he cannot ride with the wave of consecration."*

84

CHAPTER 8

CHALLENGED TO
CHANGE

"I beseech you therefore, brethren, by the mercies of God, that you present your bodies a living sacrifice, holy, acceptable to God, which is your reasonable service. And do not be conformed to this world, but be transformed by the renewing of your mind, that you may prove what is that good and acceptable and perfect will of God." (Romans 12:1-2)

The rituals of sacrifices, services and offerings to God will be a meaningless exercise if the heart is not willing to follow through to obey God in total surrender to his word. God wants us, especially his children, to consecrate our lives unto him. This includes our bodies. God demands our compliance to his word or else our worship will be mere lip service. Consecration is a command from God. It is not man's idea, and it is not optional. Think about this:

"Then said Jesus to those Jews which believed on him, If ye continue in my word, then are ye my disciples indeed". - John 8:31(KJV)

Living a lifestyle that is contrary to God's word after you became a child of God is hypocrisy. Be not deceived, you cannot fool God. He said in his word:

"Do not be deceived, God is not mocked; for whatever a man sows, that he will also reap." (Galatians 6:7)

"as obedient children, not conforming yourselves to the former lusts, as in your ignorance;
but as He who called you is holy, you also be holy in all your conduct,
because it is written, "Be holy, for I am holy." (1 Peter 1: 14-16)

Holiness is still right, and consecration is still possible in this *"adulterous, crooked and perverse generation"*. Make up your mind to give it all it takes to live holy. Disconnect your life from anything that tends to drag you to the mud of sin. Do not keep that appointment with evil, and do not visit that person or place that the enemy will take advantage of to cause you to desecrate your body through sexual immorality.

Learn how to conquer the flesh. One of the tools you can use to deal with the flesh is fasting. The energy and excitement the flesh has comes from food. As long as a man wants to please the flesh and give it all that it craves for, he cannot ride with the wave of consecration. There is no one that Satan cannot tempt sexually. The fact that you are married does not scare the devil neither does it exempt you from sexual temptation.

If he has not tempted you, or is not tempting you now, then yours is on the way, and mind you, it is not a one-time event. Thank God there is a way of escape, and consecration is that way.

"So it was, as she spoke to Joseph day by day, that he did not heed her, to lie with her or to be with her." (Genesis 39:10)

It was not God that made Joseph not to fall during his time of sexual temptation, otherwise he would be a partial God. This is because some people have fallen during their own time of temptation. All that God does for everyone of us is provide the way of escape, but it is our responsibility to escape. Joseph accepted the responsibility to use his will power and to act upon the word of God by running away.

"No temptation has overtaken you except such as is common to man; but God is faithful, who will not allow you to be tempted beyond what you are able, but with the temptation will also make the way of escape, that you may be able to bear it."
(1 Corinthians 10:13)

You need to exercise your will power. Will power is a strong determination to do, or not to do something. Your will power helps you to build a resistance against any form of temptation to sin, including sexual temptation. What you want is your desire, but what you will is your decision. Your will, will not allow your emotions to becloud your sense of judgment.

87

It will not allow your fleshly desire to overcome your desire for consecration. The will power is a potent force in every human being, you don't buy it with money. It is a free gift from God. Whether you are rich or poor, black or white, God endowed everyone with it. Make use of yours in the right way today.

"But Daniel purposed in his heart that he would not defile himself with the portion of the king's delicacies, nor with the wine which he drank; therefore he requested of the chief of the eunuchs that he might not defile himself." (Daniel 1:8)

Daniel made a decision that he would rather starve to death than defile himself. The only thing you cannot do is the thing you have not willed to do. That's why the saying goes, "Where there is a will there is a way."

For example, Shadrach, Meshach, and Abednego chose to die in the burning fiery furnace of king Nebuchadnezzar than to disobey the commandments of their God. (Daniel 3) God in his law commanded us not to make any graven image or bow down to them (Exodus 20:4-5), just like he commanded us not to commit immorality. During their dispensation a decree went forth that everyone should bow down to a graven image made by the king, contrary to the commandments they had received. There is a decree at this time in this generation from the *"Prince of this world"* (John 14:30) that all men everywhere should bow to sex, through immoral living and sexual perversion.

"Then Nebuchadnezzar in his rage and fury commanded to bring Shadrach, Meshach, and Abednego. Then they brought these men before the king. Nebuchadnezzar spake and said unto them, Is it true, O Shadrach, Meshach, and Abednego, do not ye serve my gods, nor worship the golden image which I have set up? Now if ye be ready that at what time ye hear the sound of the cornet, flute, harp, sackbut, psaltery, and dulcimer, and all kinds of musick, ye fall down and worship the image which I have made; well: but if ye worship not, ye shall be cast the same hour into the midst of a burning fiery furnace; and who is that God that shall deliver you out of my hands? Shadrach, Meshach, and Abednego, answered and said to the king, O Nebuchadnezzar, we are not careful to answer thee in this matter. If it be so, our God whom we serve is able to deliver us from the burning fiery furnace, and he will deliver us out of thine hand, O king. But if not, be it known unto thee, O king, that we will not serve thy gods, nor worship the golden image which thou hast set up. Then was Nebuchadnezzar full of fury, and the form of his visage was changed against Shadrach, Meshach, and Abednego: therefore he spake, and commanded that they should heat the furnace one seven times more than it was wont to be heated. And he commanded the most mighty men that were in his army to bind Shadrach, Meshach, and Abednego, and to cast them into the burning fiery furnace. Then these men were bound in their coats, their hosen, and their hats, and their other garments, and were cast into the midst of the burning fiery furnace." - Daniel 3:13-21 (KJV)

We are in this battle together, let us encourage one another. In case you see me hanging around the 'den,' please raise your red flag, I will not be offended. Let us be our brothers' keepers. I've got your back and you've got mine.

89

Therefore, join me in this crusade to mobilize the younger generation and prepare them for a great future. I would like to leave you with this final admonition from the word of God as found in the book of first Corinthians chapter ten in verse twelve. It says,

" Therefore let him who thinks he stands take heed lest he fall."

May the Lord keep you and uphold you to the very end in Jesus name. Amen! God bless you.

The final word:

YOU MUST BE BORN AGAIN:

Jesus said, "Marvel not that I said unto thee, Ye must be born again." (John 3:7). God created everyone on earth, but it is not everyone that is a child of God. Natural birth brings us into our different families on earth but spiritual rebirth or being born again takes us into God's family, (Romans 9:6-8).

We cannot earn salvation because all our righteousness is like a filthy rag in the sight of God (Isaiah 64:6). Salvation is by grace through faith in Jesus as the son of God and all he lived and died for (Ephesians 2:8). Neither is there salvation in any other: for there is none other name under heaven given among men, whereby we must be saved (Acts 4:12). Jesus said unto him, I am the way, the truth, and the life: no man cometh unto the father but by me (John 14:6). Jesus, his death and resurrection, is the sum total of God's plan for man's salvation.

DECISION TIME:

Accepting Christ or rejecting him is the only one decision we make here on earth that determines our eternal destiny. In other words, after one has died, the consequences of rejecting Christ or the benefits of accepting him follows him to eternity. Let no man deceive you. The Bible says:

"And as it is appointed unto men once to die, but after this the judgment" (Hebrews 9:22). (KJV)

As one draws his or her last breath in death, the place of final and eternal abode of his or her soul is decided. That is the day of accountability. No prayer of any man can relocate you from where you merited, heaven or hell (Luke 16:19-31). In Revelation 20:15 the bible says,

"And whosoever was not found written in the book of life was cast into the lake of fire." (KJV)

RECEIVE JESUS CHRIST THROUGH FAITH:

Have you been redeemed from the power of sin? Jesus came that through the forgiveness of your sin you might be reconciled to God. Do not allow the death of Jesus to be in vain in your life. He said in Matthew chapter eleven verse twenty-eight:

"Come unto me all ye that labor and are heavy laden, and I will give you rest." (KJV)

In John 6:37 Jesus said, *"All that the father giveth me shall come to me; and him that cometh to me I will in no wise cast out".* (KJV)

"Behold I stand at the door, and knock: if any man hears my voice and opens the door, I will come in to him, and will sup with him and he with me." (Revelation 3:20). (KJV)

The book of Romans 10:10 declares,

"For with the heart man believeth unto righteousness; and with the mouth confession is made unto salvation." (KJV)

You need to pray out the prayer below, and mean it in your heart.

PRAYER:

Dear Lord Jesus, I am a sinner, I believe you are the Son of God, you died for my sins and rose again on the third day. Forgive me. I repent of all my sins. Wash me and cleanse me with your precious blood. Deliver me from the power of sin and of Satan. I receive you right now into my heart, and into my life to be my personal Lord and Savior. Fill me with your precious Holy Spirit. Thank you dear Lord for saving my soul. I pray in Jesus name. Amen.

Congratulations, and welcome into the family of God!

OTHER PUBLICATIONS BY THE AUTHOR

The
GOSPELPOWER
VOLUME 1
Dealing with the total man: Spirit, Soul and Body

DEPARTURE
FROM EVIL

THE SEVEN KEY
PRINCIPLES TO
VICTORIOUS LIVING

JESUS
The Light of the World

DELIVERANCE

www.ingramcontent.com/pod-product-compliance
Lightning Source LLC
Chambersburg PA
CBHW071623040426
42452CB00009B/1455